In The Ring

Dog Shows, Spunk, and Leadership

In The Ring

Dog Shows, Spunk, and Leadership

SHERI YOUNG

Cover Photo: Meaghan Baxter Photography
                 Meaghanbaxterphotography.com

Makeup: Avery Side, Smudge & Smoulder
                 Smudgeandsmoulder.com

                 Gagan Brar – Brows by Gagan
                 blush-and-brows-studio.business.site

Hair: Jory Davie, jd.styling

Samoyeds: Sershan's Premiere Misha
                 White Evenk Onyx Maya

DEDICATION

For dog lovers everywhere and anyone striving to be
a better leader

CONTENTS

ACKNOWLEDGMENTS

Miracles happen when the desires of your heart align with your soul.

For me, this book happened when my deep love for God, my joy for showing Samoyeds, and my passion for leadership collided.

When spiritual principles and practices learned at a dog show are applied to leadership and mental health, the result is healing, wellness, compassion, and abundance.

I pray that you take the wisdom and teachings in this book and apply them fearlessly to your own life. Let the healing begin because we are all recovering from something.

Thank you to my friends in recovery who get me, have my back, love me with all my flaws and believe in me. Thank you for making a safe place for me to be my authentic self.

Thank you to my executive career mentors who showed me the value of honest, strategic, wise and compassionate leadership. Above all, you taught me how to treat others as I wish to be treated and I have never lost sight of that.

Thank you, Larry, and Evan, for loving and raising our Samoyeds together with me, and for supporting me on this purebred dog show and breeder journey. Thank you, Lisa Hubenig, for introducing us to the dog show world and trusting us with our Samoyed Misha.

I am eternally grateful to Anastasiya Dubrava for blessing us with White Evenk Onyx Maya and White Evenk Osman. Thank you, Dalia MicKiene, for breeding their father, Klajokliu Suo Simba, and for providing the magnificent sire, Klajokliu Suo You Rock My World, for Maya to establish our SurThrive Kennel breeding program.

Special thank you to the amazing Tai Copperthwaithe for working with Maya behind the scenes at conformation handling classes and for traveling with us to dog shows across the Canadian prairies. Thank you for helping Maya obtain her Canadian championships and first Best of Breed win.

And finally, I want to thank my beloved Samoyeds, Maya, Osman and Misha for their unconditional love and constant companionship. I love you to the moon and back.

INTRODUCTION

I'm new to the dog show world. I've loved and owned dogs all my life. And I've been a public and private executive for 40 years. What I experienced in and around dog shows blew my mind. The first thing that surprised me was how much participating in dog shows expanded my already deep love for my dogs. As a dog owner, breeder, and sometimes handler, I learned and developed a working relationship with my dogs that took joy to new levels.

My other surprise was how similar emotions and challenges I experienced in and around dog shows were to what I dealt with during my long career in business, government, and boardrooms. Dynamics around leadership, teamwork, and organizational culture were strikingly similar. I learned that what makes a strong team in the dog show ring is also what makes good and effective leaders in the business world.

This turned my mind to lessons that can be learned from our dogs and dog shows about how we need to take care of ourselves as human beings – to be the best leaders we can be – because we all bring our souls to work.

Both at dog shows and in the corporate world, leaders need to know how to deal with noise that can confuse and distract, how to handle both winning and losing, how to expand diversity, inclusion, and belonging, how to break down organizational silos, and how to improve mental health, happiness, and joy.

The best leadership starts with love in your heart for yourself and for others and who better to teach us about unconditional love than the wonderful affection, loyalty, and devotion we receive from our incredible spirit animals, our dogs.

Sheri Young
Calgary, September 2023

1

DOGS, DOG SHOWS,
AND LEADERSHIP

Partnership between dogs and people dates back thousands and thousands of years. It's no accident dogs and people bond so closely. They've relied on each other, worked together, comforted each other, and loved each other for millennia. Dogs are truly man's, and woman's, best friend.

All dog lovers know this, deeply. And dogs know this, too. Our relationship is hard wired in both our DNA. If we think about it, dogs and people can learn a lot about each other, and about leadership, which is what got me to thinking about writing this book.

As an author and a long-time executive, I came late to the dog show world. Long-time Samoyed lovers, we got our second Samoyed, Misha, in 2018 and started taking him to dog shows. A whole new world opened up!

As anyone who works with dogs knows – whether driving or herding farm animals; training to perform important service work in health care settings; doing agility or obedience work; working closely in teams in police or military service; or just spending important time together walking and playing every day – a special partnership develops between dog and person that involves trust, teamwork, loyalty, devotion, joy, happiness, and love.

At dog shows, it takes a lot of work to breed, train, groom, and exhibit a dog to compete with other dogs from the same breed, to compete with other breeds, and, if all goes well, to win a coveted white-blue-and-red ribbon as the lucky dog and handler out of hundreds, and sometimes thousands, of competitors to be Best In Show. This requires dedication, hard work, and leadership.

There's a lot to learn from dogs about what makes a successful leader and contributes to extraordinary performance by organizations. Attitude, behaviour, how you show up, mental health, value and respect are all ingredients needed to perform to the best of abilities for the dog and handler before a dog show judge.

Relationships between dogs and people are more than feeding, training, play, and exercise. This relationship is a spiritual one. It's a spiritual relationship because there's a lot of trust, devotion, and love involved. From love comes empathy, compassion, and wisdom, which are critical to effective leadership.

Dogs and people have worked side by side for a long, long time. In the Universe, we are all connected to something bigger than ourselves. Dogs and people are connected to each other, the earth around us, and there is a purpose for all of us. From the earliest time, when dogs were first domesticated, people and dogs worked together for common goals, to hunt and survive. There's a reason why we call dogs spirit animals. Dogs are intuitive, sensitive, and read their human partners without needing to talk, without judgment, and without having to write a report. Dogs read our faces, our moods, and our body language. They sense people's energy. People and dogs can feel each other's spirit in a deep and meaningful way.

Dog shows can be a miniature version of the corporate world. There's fierce competition. There's the need to perform on command. Dogs and handlers must take good care of each other. To perform to the best of their abilities, they need to collaborate, coordinate, and have trust and confidence in each other. They need to take risks and they each need to be on top of their mental game. Most importantly, they need to enjoy each other, have a plan, and know their purpose. They need to know how to handle their anxieties and emotions. Just like in business, dogs, handlers, breeders, and owners, need to know how to deal with both winning and losing, how to be professional, and how to demonstrate good sportsmanship, strong ethics, and positive values.

Dog shows can teach a lot about courage, leadership, and spiritual connection. We just have to open our hearts, confront challenges with an accepting mind, and be willing to learn new things. There's no limit what unconditional love flowing from our dogs can teach us about life, leadership, and spirituality.

2

NOISE

NOISE! There's a lot of noise at dog shows. The kind you hear physically with your ears, and invisible noise that bombards your head!

Dogs barking. Audience murmurs and gasps. Applause. More dogs barking. The dragging of chairs, scraping across bare floors. The constant hum of blowers drying wet dogs. Gates and cages slamming shut. Ring stewards shouting numbers. And it goes on. Dog shows are noisy.

Breeders, owners, and handlers rush through crowded spaces, maneuvering dogs of all shapes, sizes, and breeds in and out of show rings. There's a lot at stake. For the owner handler, their dog is the love of their life, and it matters a lot to get recognized by a judge. People pay big bucks to show their dogs across the country.

Needless to say, dog shows are intense environments, not unlike some workplaces. Lots of things happen all at once. If you let your mind drift off, or allow the noise to overwhelm you, you can easily miss your opportunity. If you're nervous, confused, or anxious, you're in big trouble because the spirit animal at the end of your lead feels everything.

At dog shows, you get both good wishes and bad vibes from people. It's a complex environment with lots of issues at play.

Emotions run high at dog shows and this is some of the noise you can't hear. Judges, breeders, professional handlers, owner handlers, show officials and exhibitors have a lot at stake. Training, travel, equipment and of course time and effort to raise dogs themselves all cost a lot.

Everyone covets the top prize, Best in Show. There's only one Best in Show at the end of a competition out of hundreds, and sometimes thousands, of dogs and handlers who are entered. The winner doesn't get decided by a time, a distance, a score, or a goal. Best in Show is ultimately decided by just one person, the judge, and their opinion. It's an opinion that doesn't get explained or justified.

So, what on earth do dog shows have to do with leadership? A lot actually because the common denominator is people. Spiritual beings having a human experience. We're all connected by a power greater than ourselves, and you can sense how people feel about what you're doing.

As a leader, your success is determined by how you behave, what you think, and how you deal with people. To achieve the best outcome, you must rise above noise and chaos to be true to yourself, your values, and your purpose.

And this is where the dog show environment teaches us invaluable leadership skills.

Know Your Why

Know your why. What is your plan and purpose for your life and what you're leading? If your why is clear, and your leadership is aligned with your soul, you feel peace, confidence, and serenity. So, when there's a lot of noise and chaos around you, you know in your gut things will work out as they should and there's no need to have anxiety or panic.

At a dog show, you know why you want to partner with a magnificent animal to show him or her at their very best. You want your dog to shine, showing its wonderful personality, character and energy for the world to see. You may not win, but you know your team – your dog, handler, trainer, and groomer – did their very best.

Your path in life is not straight. You have ups and downs, successes and failures, good times, and bad times. Regardless of the winding way of life, you survive and thrive in all situations when you know your WHY.

It's like a beacon in your soul that gives you hope and shines a spotlight on any chaos and darkness that comes your way. To find your why, ask the God of your understanding to reveal it to you. Search for the answers in the quiet place in your soul, and Divine love will reveal your path to you. Your life has a purpose for this place and time, and when you know that, noise and distractions cannot knock you off your game!

Stay True To Yourself and Purpose

Stay true to yourself and focus your thoughts and life on your purpose and goals. You are what you think and what you focus your mind on, you grow.

So, if your show dog isn't winning, or your office project is going sideways, remember your why and stay true to yourself. Focus on the positive things that are happening. See the possibilities through the noise, be brutally honest with yourself about how you show up to play, and visualize the success of your goals. Rise above the chaos and be grateful for the things you cannot see.

You know as a spiritual being having a human experience, there's a power greater than yourself that wants the best for you in every area of your life. All things work together for good to them that love God.

So, shut out the noise, get quiet, and connect to your Higher Power with prayer, meditation and the spiritual practice that works for you.

Choose Joy

We only have this present moment. Live in the now, connect to the essence of you and a power greater than yourself. Feel love in your soul and send it out to those you interact with, especially those who behave badly and are mean to you. Let it go. Don't assume their intentions. You don't know what people are going through.

What you give you receive. This is the law of the Universe – the law of attraction. So, when the noise around you tries to suffocate you with negativity, shift your attention to love and joy in your life. Centre your thoughts on your why, your plan and purpose, and be grateful that people, places, and situations are lining up automatically to serve you. You will notice how seamless things are when you're answering your calling and no longer fighting against life.

Be confident and centred on your why, constantly refresh and improve your plan to achieve your goals and be grateful in the present moment for the things you cannot see. Faith is the evidence of things unseen and people's opinions of you have no consequence.

Be gracious with your team and practice joy when you interact with others. Live in the moment and appreciate the blessings in your life today.

Finally, about the dog show, you may not win the coveted Best in Show prize, but you live your best life. You get to take home the best furry prize ever and spoil them with love and attention! In my humble opinion, it doesn't get any better than that!

3

WHAT IS WINNING?

E veryone loves a winner!

Everyone wants to win.

In it to win it!

Number 1. Top of the heap. Win the race. Fastest. Strongest. Score the most goals, the most points, or the least faults or mistakes.

At a dog show, the winner is Best In Show. Out of hundreds, or even thousands, of dogs entered from dozens and dozens of different breeds, Best In Show is literally the top dog, the one judges select to be superior to all of the other dogs entered.

The thrill of winning is undeniable. To cross the finish line first, hoist the Stanley Cup, or hold the Super Bowl trophy is an experience of a lifetime. Celebrating hard work, achievement, and sacrifice produces a flood of emotion, happiness, and relief.

But what is winning, really?

Winning is being spiritually awake, present in the moment and understanding life happening around you, whether you're at work or at the dog show.

Being present in the moment grounds you in your purpose, your path and the true essence of you.

Being aware of your circumstances, whether you win the ribbon or close the sale, you are uplifted knowing your truth for this space and time. Everything will work out as it's meant to be.

Winning is knowing the meaning for your life and trusting the process. The penultimate prize is your soul's vital spiritual connection to a power greater than yourself. This completes you and fills you with joy.

Don't get me wrong. Winning the prize is awesome and great fun. It's exhilarating, an adrenaline rush and a tsunami of happiness. Especially when you've been working extremely hard trying to win for a very long time.

Dog shows are a competitive environment. At a dog show, there can be thousands of entered dogs, but there's only one Best in Show. But really, all the dogs are winners because they show up and make an effort. For years behind the scenes, they do the work and make the sacrifice. They learn to perform, tolerate incessant grooming and collaborate with their human, taming their inner beast.

Besides the top dog, what about all the other dogs and their owners? Are they less worthy? I don't think so. Just like the private sector and business, it can be a dog-eat-dog world! For those fortunate enough to be awarded the top prize, it can be the event of a lifetime – an absolutely incredible achievement.

But it's temporary. It's a finite event. The glory comes and goes quickly. You get satisfaction and adulation for a moment which is fantastic. But in an instant, the recognition and notoriety is gone. When it's over you feel empty inside again. When you pass on from this life, you don't take the prize and win with you.

And therein is the challenge with "winning." It's wonderful to win, and your Higher Power wants the very best for you, but winning or losing doesn't define who you are.

That's because you are a spiritual being having a human experience and your soul is craving for a connection to a power greater than yourself. Nothing but intimacy with your Creator will fill this part of you.

To win, you must first look inward for your self-worth, fulfillment, and satisfaction.

When you're spiritually connected and true to yourself – that is winning.

Winning is actually not needing to win. That's right. You win when you know you have everything you need within you to live, not just surviving, but thriving in life.

Get Quiet And Connect

Winning is getting quiet and shifting your attention from the distractions of this world and connecting to your heart, the true essence of you. Winning is surrendering your ego and self-will to the Universe and connecting to your Creator.

This links you to the infinite, eternal part of you that transcends any worldly or competitive situation. The quiet, secret place in your heart makes you aware of who you truly are, revealing the reason why you are alive on Earth, at this place and time.

As a leader, this enables you to rise above your circumstances and see the big picture of the confluence of issues at play. The confidence you have in knowing who you are, your capability and your role, gives you grace and compassion for your colleagues and staff, and Divine wisdom to guide your decision making.

Taking a moment and getting quiet at the dog show, or at your workplace, centres you on your mission and connects you to your soul. Nothing negative can penetrate that.

Have Joy

To live a happy life, your joy must come from within. Life is really hard and there are wins and losses. So even when you don't win the prize at the dog show, or things are going south at your workplace, you still deserve to be happy and have joy.

As a spiritually wakened person, you know there's a specific plan for your life and that the ups and downs are part of the journey. There's a reason for everything that happens to you. So, even though you may not understand why you're having difficulty at work, or why you keep losing at the dog show, you know your Higher Power loves you and is holding you close. There is nothing more wonderful and amazing on Earth than this. Have faith. Get quiet and connect through your spiritual practices and feel the joy of the Universe delighting in you.

Winning is being able to experience joy, even when life isn't fair, and having the ability to be happy and gracious, even when you don't win the prize.

Know Your Purpose

Your calling in life is bigger than a Best in Show trophy or making millions of dollars in the business world. Those things are nice, and congratulations if you've achieved them, but they don't complete you and make you whole as a person.

Your calling, your role for this space, place and time, is the reason why you are conscious and breath. When you figure this out for yourself, this is nirvana and heaven on Earth. No material gain or prize can replace this feeling of completeness and love. You are hard wired to be connected to a loving presence outside of yourself.

These truths sustain you through all life situations and make you resilient. You are a winner, regardless of your outer circumstances.

This is your journey to joy.

Winning in life is being the Best You!

4

WHAT IS LOSING?

What is Losing?

There's a lot of losing at dog shows. For every dog show, which can include hundreds, if not thousands of dogs, only one gets to be Best in Show.

Losing at dog shows can teach a lot about how leaders can become great leaders through their own losses – whether it's a failure to get a promotion, losing a contract, a betrayal or the failure of a business deal.

It's tough to be brave and lead after suffering a setback. It's natural to experience self-doubt, have a momentary lapse in self-confidence and question your direction.

Remain confident, remember who you are, and see the situation for what it is, just another step on your road to ultimate success.

Competition at dog shows is fierce. Each dog, owner and handler are on their own, unique path to achieve a championship. They all start out with no points and compete against other dogs of the same sex that are building points towards a championship. The judge selects the best male, the best female and these two go on to compete against other dogs that already achieved their championships and more.

From this ring, the judge selects the Best of Breed, as well as others including Best of Opposite Sex, Select Male, Select Female, Best of Winners among the male and female yet to achieve their championship, Best Puppy or Junior. Other selections can include Awards of Merit, and Best Veteran. Points accrue according to the numbers of dogs entered in each breed.

The dog selected Best of Breed moves on to the next ring, the Group Ring, competing against other breed winners arranged into groups. In North America, breed groups are: Sporting, Hound, Working, Terrier, Toy, Non-Sporting, and Herding. Breeds are arranged in groups by each country's national kennel club, and vary slightly in regions around the world.

Dogs compete in their respective Group Ring, and the winner from each goes on to the final ring, competing for the ultimate title of Best In Show.

These dog show rings are competitive, particularly with more popular breeds. It's not unusual to see 10 to 20 dogs competing against one another in a breed ring for the coveted title of Best of Breed. It's a process of elimination, and in these intense situations, if you're not in the right frame of mind, losing can be tough and frustrating.

Sometimes it can take a purebred dog a year or more to become a national champion, depending on the number of dogs they're competing against. In some cases, a dog can achieve a championship title in just a few shows during a weekend, if they're competing against a large number of dogs.

What transpires often depends on the luck of the draw. If you breed and compete show dogs seriously, you've likely experienced both situations. But for the one purebred dog that takes what seems forever to champion, it's a long haul, significant expense and an emotional ride. Especially when your dog gets stuck in the skunk hole – the dreaded nine points - one short of the 10 points needed to become a champion.

For every success at a dog show, there's a lot of losing along the way.

When you compete at something, you become vulnerable and take on the risk of rejection and suffering a loss.

Whether competing at a dog show or taking on a leadership role in an organization, you have a responsibility to manage your expectations, your attitude, and emotions. Keep focused on your plan and purpose, because others are counting on you. The world desperately needs leaders who deal gracefully with adversity and loss, while staying focused on their mission and maintaining their dignity.

Lean Into Spirituality

When you're a spiritually awakened leader, or competing in a dog show, your relationship with the God of your understanding grounds you and frees you from anxiety, anger, frustration and the resentment of losing. When you're spiritually connected, you know someone is watching out for you, despite what your circumstances may appear to be.

If you are passed over at the dog show or your place of work for a promotion, it's OK to acknowledge the pain and take a moment to grieve. Confusion and disbelief in your mind are normal when suffering a loss. Take a deep breath, exhale, and heal. Let go of it. Everything happens for a reason.

You may initially feel confusion and panic at your predicament, so observe the negative thoughts and let them float by like clouds in the sky. Don't focus or dwell on them. Your thoughts define you in your subconscious mind, so place your attention on hope, optimism and your knowledge of your truth. The truth is your Higher Power loves you, has a plan for your life and everything is going to work out in the end.

Don't give in to the temptation of anger, resentment, and bitterness. For the love of God, move on. Be grateful that your Higher Power is organizing the Universe for people, places and situations to align with your soul. There's a reason why you've hit a bump in the road.

Inspired Leadership Through Loss

After a loss, you may not feel valued by the dog show judges, or by your organization's management. Don't get discouraged. Focus on what you or your dog did right. A loss doesn't throw you off your game because your spiritual connection defines you, holding you steady. In this space, there's no fear or anger.

Don't permit a loss at the dog show to interfere with your loving relationship with your spirit animal. In the same vein, a professional loss can't be permitted to damage your relationship with your Creator.

Life may surprise you, even shock you, from time to time, but you're OK because you know in your gut the God of your understanding is your provider for everything you need, both personally and professionally. He is your boss, your employer, your friend and the lover of your soul. So, be grateful and shift your mind from the loss to focus on your heart's desires and what really lights you up. This may give you some clues why things didn't go as anticipated or expected.

In an organization, you're still called to perform in a leadership role and serve others despite experiencing a loss. Even though you may not understand what is happening to you, as a leader you still need to practice forgiveness, and give your staff and colleagues the benefit of the doubt. In these delicate situations, your inspiration and resiliency springs up from your soul because of who you are - a spiritually awakened connected leader.

The Essence of You

When things haven't gone as planned, and you feel shaken to your core, remember who you are and feel the goodness and potential in your soul. If a door slams shut, that means the gig is not for you! Don't be sad. Be grateful. Your life and your time on Earth are precious and if you want to be truly happy and fulfilled, you need your soul to be aligned with God's will for your life.

Be aware that your ego is going to freak out at your temporary defeat and try to drown you in self-pity. Your ego is not your friend when you've experienced a loss, so dig deep to connect with spiritual truth in your soul. Rise up and use the feelings of rejection to know and improve your higher self and be the best version of you. Your life matters and you need to be on the right path.

Remember who you are, be confident in yourself and see the situation for what it is. This is just a moment in time and in the light of eternity, what matters is what you choose to think about it and how you behave. How you react impacts everyone around you, at the dog show, at home and in your workplace.

Be mindful that as a leader, your influence on people is significant. Leaders don't get a break – everyone's watching your performance – through the good times and the bad. And it's tough. You may feel like you've been gut punched in the stomach from something that didn't work out, but you're modelling the way so you must be resilient and take the high road.

Take time to practice your daily spiritual practice of prayer and meditation. Be kind to yourself and draw your value and self-worth from Divine love in your heart. Do something that makes you happy. And do it again, until you can laugh at yourself! Connect with what makes you tick in your soul, and celebrate the essence of you. Ask God to create more of these beautiful, reflective moments in your life. Ask for guidance, direction, and recognize the God whispers. These are the signs and situations of synchronicity as your life and leadership fall into place as they should.

When the right thing comes along, you'll be so grateful for your loss which set you on the correct path. Your Higher Power guides and shapes you on your journey to joy and a loss is an insignificant bump in the road.

Another Step On The Road To Success

Whether at a dog show or leading in an organization, each loss is just another step on the road to ultimate success.

A show dog gets a brand new judge the next time they walk into a ring on their quest for championships and beyond. A leader gets another opportunity to meet a challenge, inspire a team around them, execute a mission, and achieve a goal.

Today is a brand new day, full of endless possibilities and joy. Forget about the past. Don't wallow in self-pity. Prayer and meditation will deepen your understanding of how much God loves you. Your trust in his ability to take care of you will grow exponentially, and you will feel butterflies in your soul in anticipation of the amazing things coming to your life. Teach these nuggets of wisdom in leadership and resiliency to those you lead. Model the way for them.

So, hug your dog, the love machine that can't get enough of you. There will always be another dog show to enter, a new job to apply for, more contracts to bid on and new potential business partnerships. The most important thing in all of this is that you are connected to your Higher Power, your true self, and that you are on the right path. Ask, surrender, and receive. You're hard wired to be joyful, abundant, and fulfilled in everything you do in life!

5

DOG SHOWS, DIVERSITY, AND BELONGING

There are hundreds of different kinds of dogs at dog shows and each one is special and deserves to be recognized, valued, and included.

They range in size, height, and weight from the huge Tibetan Mastiff to the tiny Teacup Poodle, and their coats vary from the beautiful double coated Bernese Mountain dogs to the regal American

Hairless Terrier. Sometimes there are white coats marked with black or brown-coloured spots, like the Dalmatian, and some are predominantly one colour, like the black Russian Terrier. Some dogs are more high maintenance than others. Most are highly energetic, playful, and sensitive. Some are more stubborn than others (hence their charm). Some breeds are ancient, dating back thousands of years, like my Samoyeds. Other breeds are very new, like the Toy Fox Terrier developed in the 1930s, or Eurasiers developed in the 1970s.

The dog show environment provides access to many worlds. They are all dogs at a dog show. But they have many different looks, a wide variety of coats, sizes, and structures, different ways of moving, and different jobs they were bred to perform. They may be all dogs, but each breed requires special care from their breeders, owners, and handlers. A low-to-the-ground Dachshund moves very differently than a towering, majestic Great Dane.

Getting to know other breeds than the one you love and are familiar with gives insights and appreciation for various points of views and new perspectives. It gives you an appreciation of where other people are coming from and increases your understanding and compassion for different likes and loves.

Accepting other people and points of view and including colleagues who are different transforms attitudes, perceptions, thoughts, and ideas. This kind of transformation can dramatically improve organizations, fostering a workplace that thrives on innovation, creativity, and mutual respect.

Getting ready to go to a dog show involves going to handling classes, where owners and handlers get to work with many dogs from other breeds. While sharpening performances for the show ring, owners and handlers get to hang out with all kinds of people and their pets, opening a window to a whole new world of diversity and belonging. These breeds, owners and handlers are all different, coming from unique backgrounds with a wide range of experiences. But they're all in it for the same reason – to perform to the very best of their abilities and celebrate their awesomeness.

All the breeds and people come together in the show ring, providing a fantastic spectacle of working together to make something bigger than their individual selves.

Dropping in on a dog show can be overwhelming and loud. The noise and chaos of dogs jumping and barking, owners and handlers frantically shuffling their dogs from ring to ring, the joy and laughter of friends and family, all work together to create the phenomenon of dog shows that puts the colour and beauty of life on vivid display.

The best way to experience a dog show, whether as a spectator, breeder, owner/handler, judge or volunteer, is to be open minded and accepting of the rich diversity of dogs. At the show, energy and excitement rise in the room when unique magnificent creatures come together and interact. Each dog and their team have own story to tell and express, creating something new in a very special moment in time. It's electric!

This is what leaders can learn from dog shows. Diversity, inclusion and belonging matters. In this Universe, we are all connected by love's DNA even though we are dissimilar. Getting curious about differences with respect and openness unleashes a transformative force inside people that can redefine, improve, and shape the workforce landscape.

Diversity means many things to different people. It can refer to the social category of people, race, gender, age or simply just the differences in an organization that can set people apart. It could be what floor someone works on, whether someone works in legal, accounting, purchasing, or production. It could be a person in a wheelchair, someone with a disability you can't see, or a certain ethnic or LGBTQ group. There are lots of ways to determine who is similar and who is different.

The challenge is people can use differences and unconscious biases to predict things about other people and judge them accordingly. People can make assumptions about the intentions of others, sometimes unfairly and without providing them the benefit of understanding, empathy, or compassion. It's easier to put people in a box and category that's familiar and comfortable.

Leaders in organizations must shift this narrative in their minds. Every human being is created equally and born into this world loved completely by a power greater than themselves. We are all spiritual beings, having a human experience, and we have a purpose and role to play in this space and time.

Leaders are phenomenal when they embrace differences, other points of view, and respect unique life experiences. Just like the grand spectacle of diversity at a dog show, differences in every day life and the workplace can be celebrated and uniqueness can be valued and respected. For leaders, this new awareness of the potential of others in unimaged ways is a paradigm shift towards nurturing an environment where everyone feels valued.

Only when leaders fully accept everyone, regardless of what they look like, where they come from or how they identify, do organizations move to a higher level, inspire change, increase their productivity, and make the world a better place.

Here are three tips to nourish and inspire diversity, inclusion, and belonging in leadership:

Become More Open And Accepting

How can a leader become more open to different people and points of view?

First, look inward for validation by loving, accepting, and knowing yourself completely. Build self-confidence and self esteem by spending time in prayer and meditation, connecting to a power greater than yourself. Optimize your self care by getting quiet. Feed your soul and ground the essence of you in Divine love.

Make a daily habit of meaningful connection to the God of your understanding. This deepens knowledge of truth, equality, and justice. Faith becomes stronger. Building a strong faith opens hearts and eyes. Open hearts bring more love, compassion, and understanding for others. Love replaces fear and insecurity.

As you step into your own truth, the talents, various points of views and differences of others no longer threaten you because you are happy, fulfilled, and complete.

You begin to view diversity in others as a genuine blessing that makes you better. You know your calling in life and the universal truth that you are a part of something bigger than yourself. This strengthens your character, makes your life purpose crystal clear and removes any fear or perceived threat from others who are different from you. Your spiritual connection opens your eyes to see the beauty, creativity, and potential in others. Everyone is fearfully and wonderfully made and has a contribution to make in this space and time.

Feel The Connection

Every human being on the planet is created by God's love and has a special role to play in the Universe. As spiritual beings having a human experience, we're all connected and loved by the God of our understanding. We're all one big magnificent, complicated, diverse human family with a spiritual connection to each other. That's why being together and caring for one another feels so much better than being alone. We need one another to be whole and healthy individuals. To be clear, unconditional love has no favourites and no person is better than the other. In the presence of your Higher Power, prejudice, bigotry, hatred, racism, or fear do not exist.

It's vitally important to feel self-confident and secure in your connection to your true self, whatever stage you're at in life. Shifting focus from human circumstances to the soul and eternal truths heightens awareness and knowledge that everyone else is created by Divine love. Suddenly, what you look like, what country you're born in, what language you speak or what you do for a living doesn't seem all that important. When you realize you're an eternal being having a human experience, and living in eternity right now, you begin to see the souls of others and feel the loving connection and empathy pulsating through us all.

Spending meaningful time with your Creator, immersed in Divine love, you become more like God himself and you instinctively feel the flow of unconditional love between people. The purpose of this loving energy is two-fold: First, it heals and restores your own soul, and second, it eliminates any hurt, anger and/or resentment you have for those who hurt you. Perfect love removes any prejudice or unconscious bias. All you feel is pure love and connection.

This Divine flow of love reshapes your mindset to be compassionate, empathetic, and understanding. You acquire the supernatural ability to let things go, accept, and cherish other peoples' differences. Compassion and empathy flows like a mighty river. Be open to change. Embrace new experiences. Welcome new people that bring different points of view, attitudes, and experiences to the table.

The best leaders recognize we're all connected and leverage that knowledge to be intuitive, wise, and compassionate. Great leaders put themselves in other peoples' shoes. They consider the impact of their decisions and unintended consequences. Self-forgiveness, self-acceptance and a good dose of humour strengthens leaders' mental health and gives them confidence to accept others different from themselves.

Drive Inclusiveness and Creativity

Inclusive leadership is a conscious choice leaders make on their spiritual journey. Inclusive leadership shapes behaviours such as courage, awareness, vulnerability, curiosity, and compassion.

When companies implement policies promoting diversity, inclusion, and belonging, productivity and profitability increase. Staff morale improves when employees feel their voices are heard. A commitment to diversity in hiring practices expands talent pools, attracting the best professionals to improve the quality of decision making and problem-solving skills.

According to Forbes Magazine, companies with a diverse workforce are 35% more likely to experience greater financial returns from their respective non-diverse counterparts. Also, companies with significant employee diversity are 70% more likely to capture more markets. Companies and organizations that implement diverse and inclusive policies attract the best talent, meet the needs of their consumers, and are better able to respond to challenges.

The best organizations and companies hold themselves accountable for results from implementing diversity and inclusion policies, actively monitoring their workforce demographic and retaining top performers so diverse talent is nurtured and not lost. These workplaces promote openness and tackle biases, discrimination, harassment, and bullying head on. Employees trust management teams that practice what they preach by ensuring diverse talent is well represented at all levels, especially among senior leaders, demonstrating fairness, transparency and enabling equal opportunity.

So, take a good look at diversity at dog shows, with dozens of breeds coming together with one purpose, celebrating their differences, and working towards one goal. We can't possibly be all the same – how boring would that be! Embrace change, welcome differences in others, and connect with each other. We are stronger when we stretch, grow, collaborate, and create our future together. Variety is indeed the spice of life!

6

BREAKING DOWN
SILOS

Imagine handling a towering, beautiful Great Dane in the ring at a dog show. It's taken a long time to master the art of showing a Great Dane to the best of the dog's ability: Learning to move quickly to showcase the dog's wonderful stride; training the dog to stand still to display its amazing structure, stance, and strength; making the Great Dane comfortable and confident in the busy dog show environment.

Now, suddenly switch leads with the handler next to you, with a diminutive Dachshund on the lead. The goal is exactly the same – present the dog to the best of its abilities to impress a judge and maybe win a ribbon. But the skills needed are very different. First of all, the Dachshund is just a few inches off the ground, as opposed to a long-legged Great Dane. The Dachshund moves at a different pace, has a different structure, and was bred to perform a very different job.

For young junior handlers in the dog show world, this is exactly the exercise they learn and display in competition. Junior handlers must learn different breeds, how they move and behave, and how to earn the dog's trust.

So, what can dog shows teach about breaking down silos in large or small organizations. Quite a lot, actually.

Like dog breeds, silos in organizations can get used to doing things in certain ways. Leaders and staff stick to their own lane, approaching problems in certain ways and executing solutions in familiar patterns.

In the workplace, silos happen a lot. When the going gets tough, people tend to hunker down and isolate to survive. Back-to-back meetings, overflowing email inboxes and looming deadlines zap morale and limit emotional bandwidth for situational awareness and compassion for colleagues.

Humans tend to isolate. Go it alone. It's part of natural survival instinct to protect and guard what people have, especially when they're under a lot of pressure.

Silos pop up in organizations at the best of times.

Leaders can learn some important lessons from junior handlers.

In the junior handler ring, where kids sharpen their dog handling skills, judges conduct an exercise that all executive and managements teams should play close attention to.

In the ring, junior dog handlers guide their dogs when the judge orders them to switch dogs. In other words, pass the dog they're leading and familiar with, ahead to their colleague, and receive the one from behind.

Can you imagine the fright! In an instant, the junior handler with the tiny Pomeranian now finds themselves with an energetic Dalmatian at the end of their lead. What are they to do?

This is a total game changer! Instantly, the junior handler has a new appreciation for what the colleague behind them had on their plate.

Here's the key takeaway: Switching leadership positions with your colleague causes a fundamental shift in perspective and gives new understanding and appreciation for one another.

Here's what leaders can learn from this dog show exercise:

Isolating is Unnatural

First, we are spiritual beings having a human experience and our brains are hard wired for a connection outside of ourselves, whether that's with spirit animals or other human beings. Isolating from the world is unnatural because people are designed to connect to a power greater than themselves, to be compassionate, understanding and patient with each other.

Connection is the operating system of the Universe. From a business perspective, connection between each other is the love spark that leads to wisdom, intelligence, and new knowledge and appreciation that informs decision-making and paths forward.

New Perspectives

Switching leadership positions with colleagues causes a fundamental shift in perspective and gives new understanding and appreciation for different roles, responsibilities, and actions.

Like getting the Great Dane and Dachshund to perform the best of their abilities, leading different teams and functions in an organization gives better appreciation for different points of views, challenges, management styles, functions, and cultures that are all necessary to come together to make a successful enterprise.

Compassion and Understanding

There's an old saying that you really don't know what a person is going through unless you walk in their shoes. In other words, before you judge them, spend some time trying to understand their experiences, perspectives, and intentions. When the junior handler switches dogs in the show ring, or when a leader moves into a different management role, it's an eye-opening experience. Assumptions are put to the test. Leaders who switch management jobs, even for a short while, increase their understanding of their colleague's business function, operational requirements, and team dynamics, realizing their assumptions about their colleagues' leadership style may have been incorrect.

Leaders don't lead alone, and research shows that shared leadership results in improved team effectiveness. Leaders who switch roles, or co-lead a team, have better appreciation and increased respect for one another as they become aware of the effort, oversight and management responsibilities of their colleagues. This builds respect, compassion and understanding for colleagues because of new awareness of the issues at play.

Well-functioning management teams work together with respect and mutual understanding to help each other. Another leader's problem becomes every team member's problem. Leaders listen to each other's difficulties and challenges, compassionately leaning in to collaborate and create innovative solutions. They rejoice and celebrate the accomplishments and achievements of each other.

So be aware of silos in your organization and have the courage of junior dog show handlers to step out of your comfort zone and take on a new area of responsibility to manage. The world is a better place when leaders collaborate and cooperate with kindness and positivity, open their hearts, and move out of their comfort zone.

Magic happens when leaders get vulnerable, break down silos and come together to form multidisciplinary teams that develop creative and powerful solutions for each other. Having the benefit of different perspectives and points of views reveals new possibilities and approaches that simply can't be developed in isolation or silos.

Just like the junior handler in the dog ring with a new dog at the end lead, they literally step into their power, go with their gut, connect with their purpose, and watch miracles happen!

7

HOW DOG SHOWS HELP YOUR MENTAL HEALTH AND SOUL

There's a lot of anxiety at a dog show.

Standing at ringside, waiting for the ring steward to call your show dog, is nerve wracking. The handler, owner, or breeder has done everything possible, training, bathing, and grooming their beloved spirit animal for this special moment.

They've got a lot in the game and there's nothing else to do now but wait for their dog's number to be called, for the show dog to happily trot by and watch the scene unfold, just like in a movie.

Despite years of thoughtful preparation, financial investment, and the tsunami of emotions an owner or breeder feels at this moment, they have absolutely no control over what's about to happen next. Entering their dog into this competition puts them in a vulnerable space. Win or lose, it's all up to the dog, the handler, and the judge.

For me, as an owner, breeder, and sometimes handler, I often feel the bottom of my stomach falling away as my dogs go into the ring. Gee – did I really think this through? I ask myself: Is this worth it? It's thrilling and terrifying and it could go either way.

For a breeder, their show dog is the result of extensive heath testing and careful consideration of pedigree and research to combine the best bitch and sire to produce a healthy litter of purebred puppies that align with national breed standards. Now at ringside, my show dogs, poofed and pampered, intuitively sense my frayed nerves. Sometimes, they bark around my ankles, circling like a cat on a hot tin roof. My connection to my spirit animals runs deep.

The range of feelings in the moment is extraordinary. We're all in human school and we learn a great deal about our mental health and the maturity of our souls by being mindful about how we show up at ringside. Challenging situations invoke intense emotions and expose the core of who we truly are.

At ringside, pause, take a deep breath and check-in with yourself. Every situation in life is an occasion to improve mental health and spirituality through the care and nurturing of your soul. The benefits and positive outcomes of this important spiritual work will make your soul stronger and more resilient.

As spiritual beings having a human experience, we frequently find ourselves at crossroads with life choices that require risk taking. Governed by the laws of time and change in the Universe, opportunities emerge as part of the normal ebb and flow of life. It's natural and very human to feel stress and apprehension when faced with uncertainty since reactions of anxiety and fear stem from primal survival instincts. But don't let these feelings get the better of you.

Acknowledge and observe intense feelings, then allow them to float away. Shift attention back to love, joy, and purpose in life. Focus on what lights you up and makes your heart sing.

At the dog competition, I sometimes freak out that I can't control the judge's decision. But I can put boundaries around my mental health by intentionally shifting focus onto our loving Higher Power who has our back and is working all circumstances for good. Be present and stand in this truth! After all, even if you don't win a prize, you get to bring the best dog home to snuggle with on the couch, or bed!

On the trajectory of life, we're all trying to figure out how to be our best selves and be happy. Uncomfortable situations provide an opportunity to pause, lift the hood and take a good look inside to make sure you're okay. Checking in with emotions could go something like this: Am I using intense, difficult situations to become my higher self, shifting my thoughts onto all things possible, or am I gripped by fear, focused on the past, stuck in a rut, depressed by current circumstances? Am I practicing soul-based leadership from a place of love, empathy, and compassion. Is my self-centered ego running my show, creating havoc, determined to win at all costs, with no regard for the feelings and emotions of others? Or am I connected to my soul, am I calm, filled with peace, serenity, and love for myself and others? Can I be happy for the success and accomplishments of my colleagues?

Build extraordinary mental strength and resilience through prayer, meditation, and fellowship with like-minded people who inspire. The way to acquire empathy, forgiveness and compassion for yourself and others comes from a daily spiritual practice and a life lived in Divine presence, connected to your Higher Power.

Showing Up

When experiencing intense emotions and situations over which you have no control, lean into spiritual connection to the God of your understanding and know you are safe and loved. A sudden rush of anxiety that numbs is a signal to immediately tether your mind and soul to your Creator.

When confronted with chaos and uncertainty, either personally or professionally, remember you are a spiritual being with an infinite soul having a human experience. There is a unique plan and purpose for your life that includes health and wellness, happiness, and abundance. You show up in life with the knowledge that you are connected to a power greater than yourself, and every situation presents valuable spiritual teachings for you. Human school constantly gives opportunities to utilize superpowers from the soul to improve mental health and wellness.

What does this look like in practice? Make kindness a habit and be non-judgmental towards others. Don't assume you know other people's intentions because you have no idea what they're feeling or going through. Rise up and be aware of your spiritual connection to the souls in your immediate vicinity, regardless of the dog their holding, their job title or paygrade. Look for goodness in others. Give them benefit of the doubt and send out love, especially when they mistreat you. Feel the presence of the God of our understanding surrounding you and know your truth.

Let Go Of Things You Cannot Control

For the benefit of mental and spiritual health, whether at a dog show, the workplace or at home with family, it's important to let go of things you cannot control and accept things you cannot change! Surrendering troubles to the Universe makes fear, worry, and anxiety dissipate. To make peace and come to terms with unfairness and uncertainty in life, trust and accept unconditional love.

Take a deep breath, exhale slowly and let go of the things you cannot control. Repeat. There's no need to worry or be anxious about anything because your Higher Power loves you and has your back. You are complete in the presence of Divine love, which is actively working your circumstances for your good. And there will likely be some winning and losing along the way to make your soul more resilient. Don't despair!

Part of letting go involves trusting the Universe with timing. There's a time for winning, and there's a time for losing. There's a time for sadness, and a time for joy. The journey of life through space and time is between you and your Creator. You may not understand the timing, but you aren't stressed or anxious because you know it's impossible for Divine love to fail you. So, cowboy up and have faith, patience and gratitude.

Who knew the true meaning of life can be revealed at a dog show?

8

WHAT DOGS TEACH ABOUT LOVE

Unconditional love from our dogs teaches us how to open our hearts to do extraordinary things and be our highest selves. Your spirit animal will do anything for you in a heartbeat. An excellent way to start every morning is snuggling with your dog and breathing in pure love.

A tsunami of unconditional love flows from your cherished dog with no strings attached. Love is the most important thing in life. Don't overcomplicate it. Just like the air you breathe; you can't live without it.

You are healthier and more fulfilled when you allow your canine guardian angel to teach you how to be more compassionate, kind and spiritually aware. Your Higher Power loves you through your bond with your dog. Your dog is delivering a very important message that you are deeply loved by the God of your understanding who has a plan and purpose for your life in this space and time.

Effective, dynamic, and compassionate leadership stems from a place of love. And, in order to love others, whether it's your family, friends, colleagues, or the people you lead, you must first love and make peace with yourself.

Imagine a world where leaders hug their dogs and connect to their Higher Power every morning, positioning themselves to make intelligent, common-sense decisions based on compassion, empathy, and justice. Leaders are uniquely positioned to have significant impacts on communities, sectors, and market economies in trillions of different ways.

A leader's decision to tether their soul to Divine love activates the Universe's system of synchronicity, which places a leader at the right place at the right time. There is no such thing as "coincidence" when the God of your understanding guides your path and shapes your affairs. People, places, and situations organize around your leadership and activities for your benefit. Your way in professional and personal life becomes clear, and your happiness and joy soar. You see your Higher Power's vision, plans and purpose for your life and all things become possible.

Welcome to the miracle zone of leadership! A leader becomes intuitive and wise beyond their natural human capacity when their soul aligns with their Creator. They perceive life happening around them through the light of eternity and the prisms of their infinite souls. They sense trends, motivations and issues at play that cannot be seen by the naked human eye. Their supernatural gifts of wisdom and insight are balanced by a burning desire in their hearts to serve others and make the world a better place. Drawing on the intelligence, wisdom and power of love in their awakened hearts, they make soul-based decisions.

Love is ground zero for your relationship with your Creator, yourself, and the world around you. All the wisdom, intelligence, and mysteries of the Universe stem from Divine love. And it so happens that this magnificent, mystical love of creation flows abundantly through every dog on the planet, whether they're show dogs, a cherished pet, or living wild on the street. Perfect love, with no earthly limitations, connects you to your furry best friend whose purpose is to bring healing and joy to your life.

Your Higher Power loves you through your bond with your dog. You are healthier and more fulfilled when you allow your canine guardian angel to teach you how to be more compassionate, kind, patient, and spiritually aware.

Spiritual beings having human experiences are hard wired to connect to love, a power greater than themselves. Make a spiritual connection stronger by asking your Creator to reveal himself to you as you surrender your ego and self-will to his care. Divine love heals hearts, awakens souls, and reveals true purpose. What you do for a living, what you own and what you accomplish in this world does not define who you really are.

Clarity on how to live a happy healthy life and be an effective compassionate leader comes from being spiritually awake, tethered to Divine love. Spirituality provides self-love, self-worth, confidence, and understanding about how to lead authentically from a happy place.

Nurturing your soul, and connecting with your true self, brings insight, imagination, empathy, and wisdom required for extraordinary leadership and a fulfilling human experience. Love, wisdom, and spiritual awareness define your leadership and human journey.

Great leaders are humble and vulnerable, courageously working on themselves to be healthy and whole. To be compassionate, they must first have compassion for themselves. To forgive others, they must forgive themselves. To bring healing to others, they must heal themselves. Connecting to their Higher Power, they dispel any fear, anger, resentment, self-pity and jealousy from their hearts and consciousness to allow Divine love, compassion, and wisdom to flow freely through them to their colleagues and the people they lead.

Hug your furry friend and accept unconditional love into your heart. The source of your dog's love is your Creator, the God of your understanding, who has always, and will always, love and be with you for eternity.

Your spiritual connection is the gateway to healing to be the best version of you. As you become healthier, you'll be able to share your experiences to give hope and improve the lives of others. As Divine love heals your soul, this loving spirit will spill out onto those around you. You are called to love others as you love yourself.

That's all you need to know. Surrender, put your Creator in control and align your soul with your true purpose. Be grateful for your journey. Just hold the face of your dog in your hands and look deeply into those eyes. Love has all the answers.

9

MAKE JOY A HABIT

Does your dog fill your heart with joy? Does he make your heart sing in a way no one else can? Does he light you up, making you laugh and not take life so seriously?

The joy you feel from your dog heals, restores, and makes your path clear. Your amazing spirit animal supports and loves you unconditionally. Together, you can handle anything life throws at you. The simple daily habit of practicing joy with your dog puts you in Divine presence. Being joyful with your dog is a superpower that lifts you up, gets you out of your head, and connects you to the God of your understanding.

Leaders who recognize lessons their dogs can teach about love, teamwork, partnership, loyalty, devotion, and joy can do extraordinary things. These leaders are compassionate, intuitive, and wise, drawing on spiritual awareness to guide, reveal insights, and shape decisions and actions.

Joy is a natural state. Joy is part of your primary purpose because joy spreads love throughout the world through you. As a spiritual being having a human experience, you are hardwired to live a joyful, abundant life.

The best leadership comes from a place of joy. Effective and transformative leaders inspire others to be happy and enjoy what they are doing in their organizations. A joyful leader sees people and values them. Joy and laughter improve morale and organizational culture, leading to deeper and more meaningful professional relationships that build trust and confidence.

Remember, we are spiritual beings in human school, and our brains are hard wired for a transcendental experience bigger than ourselves. Human beings are designed to live life connected with the God of their understanding. This spiritual connection is ground zero for joy.

Joy is a choice, so make joy a habit, regardless of circumstances. If you need help shifting your mind away from challenging situations, give your furry friend a hug, take him for a walk or go throw the ball with him. When you shift attention toward a happy experience, you connect to your Higher Power and feel joy on a whole new level.

Medical research identifies significant health benefits from joy and happiness. Studies reveal physical benefits, including a stronger immune system, stronger resilience in the face of stress, a stronger heart, and less risk of cardiovascular disease. Being joyful contributes to quicker recovery times from illness or surgery.

Research also suggests joy and happiness can help us live longer. Joy improves mental and emotional health. Just imagine the positive impact joy could make in your workplace or in your family life, if everyone showed up with joy in their hearts!

So, make joy a habit. Whatever that looks like for you.

Get into action today and do things that bring you joy and make you happy. When you put joy into practice, it deepens your relationship with yourself and your Higher Power. It's taking self-kindness and self-compassion to a new level, helping you to get better. Joy is infectious. We're all connected and when you send your joy out to those around you, whether it's at the dog show, your workplace or at home, you make a positive impact on others, and you get boundless amounts of joy back in return.

A daily joyful practice could be a million different things. It could be listening or dancing to music, doing a craft, building a business, volunteering at a food bank, enjoying the outdoors or spending time with your kids and grandkids. Or it could even be entering a dog show. Do whatever lights you up and makes you feel great! And do it again and again!

The more deliberate joy you create, the more joy you attract to your life. You're like an antenna, welcoming people, places, and situations that align with your true calling in life. The intentional act of joy connects your soul with Divine love, the true essence of you and your purpose in life.

Be joyful for who you are and what you have. Be aware you are what you think. Don't focus on what you feel you're lacking. Change your mindset from scarcity to a positive perspective and be grateful for what you have now.

You exponentially create more abundance when you make joy a habit. This is the law of attraction. Abundance comes as you focus on your blessings, when you are grateful for your experiences, and when you realize your Higher Power's plan for your life.

Be joyful and grateful for the things that you've asked your Higher Power for. Feel joy and contentment for the things coming to you that are still unseen, and act like you've already received them. This is the power of unwavering faith, as synchronicity kicks into high gear and organizes people, places, and situations to support you in fulfilling your life purpose.

That's why you need to be grateful today for your circumstances and choose to celebrate with joy what you have. Believe in yourself and have courage.

When you make joy a daily habit, you connect with the true essence of you. Your positive energy and feelings of joy that you experience when you hug your dog immerse you in your Creator's love for you.

Your joyful daily spiritual practice unlocks the secrets of why you exist and who you are. Enjoy and delight in getting quiet and nurturing your soul. To share your life with your dog, and love each other unconditionally, is a life well lived. Your circumstances will rise up to meet you and support you on your journey to joy. Your delightful spirit animal connects you directly to the power of creation! God help us to simply open our hearts and receive unconditional love.

ABOUT THE AUTHOR

Sheri thinks deeply about spirituality, how to strengthen her connection to the God of her understanding, and how to help and serve others.

A spiritually awakened recovering alcoholic, Sheri strives to shine light and love on everything that crosses her path in life, seeking spiritual truth and increased understanding.

Living a Samoyed life expanded her horizons to dog shows, a Samoyed breeding program and wonderful new friendships in the dog community.

An author and speaker, Sheri takes more than 40 years of executive leadership experience in the public and private sector and applies it to the very human experience of participating in a dog show. Drawing on her passion for both dogs shows and effective leadership, Sheri identifies the similarities in human emotions and behaviours to teach best practices and spiritual lessons for making better leaders and improving mental health and wellness.

When Sheri is not cuddling, walking, training, and picking up after her Samoyeds, she can be found searching for peace and serenity on her boat on Okanagan Lake, spending time in the Canadian

Rockies, or putting prayer and meditation into daily spiritual practice.

Sheri holds a BA (Political Science) from Carleton University, as well as a post-graduate BAA (Journalism) from Ryerson University. Sheri also holds the ICD.D designation from the Institute of Corporate Directors, Rotman School of Business, University of Toronto.

ABOUT SURTHRIVE SAMOYEDS

Sharing life with Samoyeds brings joy, love, happiness and celebrates magnificent creatures. Samoyeds are truly spirit animals. An ancient breed thousands of years old, Samoyeds live and work closely with people. Samoyeds herd, pull, love and play with intelligence and huge hearts.

At SurThrive Samoyeds, registered with the Canadian Kennel Club, we raise, breed, promote and show our dogs to share our love for these special creatures, spreading the joy they bring into a Samoyed life.

Samoyeds are happiest when they share their lives closely with their humans. Living a Samoyed life means being active with your Samoyeds. They need a job to do. Very smart, they bore easily and need constant partnership, communication, and love from their families. A vocal dog, their shrill bark was meant to communicate across vast Arctic landscapes, like when their tribe dispatched a Samoyed to find a lost reindeer and called to say they found the wayward animal.

A Samoyed is truly a spirit animal. They read their masters' moods and feelings. When you dance, Samoyeds laugh and dance with you. Working closely with people makes them happiest, and they form deep, life-long bonds. A Samoyed will pick his special person, and they will be friends forever.

Samoyeds are all love, all the time, always speaking with you, bringing joy into your life.

Learn more about our kennel at
https://SurThriveSamoyeds.life/

OTHER BOOKS BY SHERI YOUNG

Relapse Roller Coaster
Alcoholic Delusion to Spiritual Clarity

Sheri first explored the power of a strong spiritual connection as she grappled with addiction to alcohol.

For readers who cannot stop drinking, this book is about relapse, and how to get off an endless roller coaster of pain, despair, and addiction. Human beings share one thing in common – a soul. Any solution to alcoholism must address the spiritual condition.

Your Spiritual Gift

Sheri dives deeper into spirituality, examining how to strengthen our connection to the God of our understanding, and how to get into daily practice to seek clarity, nurture the soul and allow Divine love to flow through life. In this book, Sheri explores spirituality through nature and connecting with the flow of love in nature.

Available on Amazon

CONTACT THE AUTHOR

Sheri frequently shares more thoughts on spirituality and connecting with each other at www.SurThrive.Life.

You can connect with Sheri through social media on:

Instagram at https://www.instagram.com/surthrive.life/

Facebook at https://www.facebook.com/SurThrive.life

X, formerly Twitter, at https://twitter.com/SurthriveL

SurThrive Samoyeds are also very busy on social media. Follow the latest fun on:

YouTube at SurThrive Samoyeds - YouTube

Instagram at
https://www.instagram.com/surthrivesamoyeds/

Facebook at
https://www.facebook.com/SurThriveSamoyeds/

X, formerly Twitter, at https://twitter.com/sur_thrive

Readers can also reach Sheri directly by e-mail at
Sheri@SurThrive.life